Scott Hilton's CREDIT SECRET

Okay first thing's first. My loophole works 100% of the time when used correctly. And there is absolutely nothing the banks can do about it, except try to control us through fear and intimidation.

Let's both agree right now, that we're not going to allow them to do that.

I need you to commit to my method, all the way through.

All we are doing is using one tiny little law in our favor, via strategic correspondences and timelines that will allow YOU to flip the script, and put the banks under YOUR control.

And trust me, this is far more powerful than what most credit repair companies do. We are not going to simply write letters, disputing our debts, and hope for the best. Shockingly, that is what every single credit repair firm has done, anytime I've hired them.

All it takes is a bit of time, focus, and a willingness to "push through" when the banks (and credit bureaus) ultimately attempt to make you fear them (by a phone call or letter).

Do not fear them. You are in control. And shortly, they will fear you... and give you whatever you want, just to go away. (sometimes this even includes CASH)

I wouldn't be surprised if you get some apologies, and some compensation for your "troubles". Because once we are through, they will be begging you to go away.

I am excited for you!

My guess is, you will be getting some pre-approved credit offers in the mail very soon, with LOW interest rates.

Your life is about to change in a big way my friend. I can't wait to hear about your success story!

OK. Let's get started with getting your credit life back on track.

- Scott & Alison

⋆ IMPORTANT NOTES ⋆

• Please follow my method from start to finish, step by step. And do not skip ahead, or you risk missing a key element that could be the decisive factor in your success or failure.

• Make sure you are well organized. I recommend file folders, and keeping reminders on your cell phone for very important cutoff dates. Keeping track of who got what, and who replied or didn't, is essential.

• Our goal is to become "not worth it" for banks and credit bureaus. We will show them we know the law. We will point out exactly how they broke it (which we will make sure they do). And they can either remove our bad credit or pay us damages (or both). Fortunately, with my guide, you will be able to quickly make it known to the banks and credit bureaus that they will find it much more advantageous to simply remove your bad credit, and quickly. :)

• My method is extremely effective, and can be used for "bad", if it gets in the wrong hands. Please promise me, that after your credit is fixed, you will NOT go back into your old bad habits. If you intend to purposely defraud a bank or financial institution, by applying for a credit card or loan that you know you cannot pay back, simply because you know that you can just re-use my method to erase it again... I have a problem with that. I am here to help you, and your past mistakes. But I do not want this method abused. Please only proceed if you agree.

• You may want to enlist another member, or a friend or family member to help you stay accountable. It is easy to get distracted with life, and miss important action items in your credit repair process. I highly recommend that you visit our private Facebook Group and interact with others in our community, to learn from them, and for encouragement.

• Make sure you ask questions in the Facebook Group and read our FAQ at the end of this guide. If you have a question that isn't answered there, you can submit a support ticket at support.creditsecret.org.

• And PLEASE... once you have success... send us an update at the HELP DESK or post it in our Facebook Group. This helps to motivate others and allows you to pay it forward!

Scott Hilton's

CREDIT SECRET

TABLE OF CONTENTS

The Credit Bureaus:
Where to reach them, and what to say. (and what NOT to say)............................. 5

Your Credit Report:
Where to get them, and exactly what to do with them... 6

What to Do with Your Credit Reports and Scores:
Jump right in and be on your way to a huge credit score increase within the next 24 hours! Step by Step, using my loophole... 7

Just Do This:
My loophole in full effect. My entire 3 part process... 8

Pre-Written Letters to Send in Any Scenario:
Not your average letters!.......................... 12

Small Claims:
How to scare the pants off of a collector, creditor, or credit bureau.......... 31

Quickly Get 3 Good Credit Lines:
How to get 3 great credit lines within 30 days... 34

Final Notes / Summary:
Wrap up of important notes.................... 35

What to do After My Method Fixes Your Credit:
Tips from a FICO officer.......................... 36

Frequently Asked Questions:
Always check here before submitting a support ticket... 37

Proof this Works:
Here are some happy members............... 41

*Disclaimer: I am not a lawyer, and none of my advice, instructions or tips should be construed as legal advice. You are responsible for any actions you take (or do not take). I will not be held responsible for any losses you incur financially, physically, or mentally. Although I have never had anyone learn my materials and incur any damages or losses whatsoever, and it is extremely unlikely, my attorney wants me to include this legal mumbo jumbo, just in case something weird happens. If you agree, then please continue. If you disagree, do not use my materials.

THE CREDIT BUREAUS

There are 3 credit bureaus that matter. They are:

Experian
P.O. Box 4000
Allen, TX 75013

Equifax Credit Information Services, Inc.
P.O. Box 740256
Atlanta, GA 30374

TransUnion, LLC
P.O. Box 2000
Chester, PA 19022

*****Do not contact them at all until you have gone through this guide completely.*****

I have deliberately omitted the phone numbers and websites of each credit bureau above, because you should NEVER dispute anything with them via online forms or phone. We will only communicate with them via regular postal mail. The reason is, it gives them less time to respond. And many times that means they have already broken the law by not responding in time. That is the easiest way possible to beat them, but just one of the many ways I will show you.

(*by the way, as a sidenote, postal mail is GREAT – did you know that if you file a paper tax return by mail, you are much less likely to be audited than those who e-file? – I know it's off topic, but that is something to think about – okay back to repairing your credit)

What's interesting to note is that you may have some bad credit only showing with one of the credit bureaus, or you may have GOOD credit only showing with one of them. This is because lenders do not always report to all 3 credit bureaus. You will find that you have 3 different credit scores, and they may be a lot different from one another. So it is important that we first find out exactly what is reported at all three bureaus, so we know exactly what you're dealing with.

And it is also very important that we keep very close track of the dates as we begin this process. So we need to not only download your latest 3 credit reports and scores, but we also need to print them out, because it will give you a hard copy that is dated. The date will be a major factor we will use against the credit bureaus very soon. Just keep that in mind.

Also, I will tell you that the ONLY reason you will NOT succeed, is due to inaction. If you follow the guide exactly, you will do great. If not, you won't. Just do the work! It's that simple.

YOUR CREDIT REPORT

Where to Get Your 3 Credit Reports & Scores

You've probably seen tons of tv commercials and ads online, with catchy jingles about "free credit reports".

What they don't mention is that your "free" report is typically only free for a few days, and then they begin auto-charging your credit card something like $30 per month until infinity – AND they make you call to cancel, instead of being able to do it online. This is because their office may be closed, or they will put you on hold forever, hoping you'll give up and get charged again. Or, because they have phone representatives who are trained to try and "re-sell" you, convincing you to stay with them for a brief discount. For example, they may offer to give you one month free. But they know most people will just forget after that, and get auto-charged again after the free month is over.

That is why they ask for your credit card when downloading your "free" report. Another thing is, they usually only show you one report and one score, but you don't get the others. Or they may show you all 3 reports, but no scores. It can become annoying and frustrating, and the dollar amounts will start to add up if you aren't careful.

I only use one service to get all 3 of my credit reports, and all 3 of my free credit scores.

http://creditsecret.org/scores/

Now keep in mind, they do ask for your credit card, but they will only charge you a fee if you decide to stay a member after the 7 day trial.

For my loophole to work perfectly, you will need to continue to be a member with Free Score Finder for at least 30 days, and preferably 60 days. It will be WELL WORTH their small fee, to get everything you need in one nicely organized place.

My method will work quickly, but no matter what, we will need to check all 3 of your credit reports and scores again in 30 days just to make sure that all of your negative info has been removed. If they haven't been removed, you have proof that the credit bureaus or your creditors broke the law.

So we just need to make sure your score has gone up, and that the credit bureaus and your creditors have fulfilled on their obligations.

I will explain all of this in more detail below, step by step. But for now, just trust me - you need to go ahead and get your 3 most recent credit reports and free scores here:

http://creditsecret.org/scores/

And once you have done so, you may continue to the next page.

Scott Hilton's CREDIT SECRET

WHAT TO DO WITH YOUR CREDIT REPORTS AND SCORES

The 3 items we are concerned with most are:

- "Public Records"
- "Derogatory Accounts"
- "Unsatisfactory Accounts"

All of these are bad, and in that order.

1) Public records are the worst – these include bankruptcies, tax liens, judgments, and other items of "public record" that other people can see.Typically when you have a public record, you will get inundated with letters from lawyers who promise to help you. I would recommend throwing those in the trash. These are usually from shady lawyers who purchased your information from the credit bureaus, in order to try to sell you their expensive and useless services. They will try to scare you. Ignore them. The more creative guys will send you letters that look hand written. They aren't. They don't care about you, so again, toss these letters and don't give them a second though.

2) Derogatory accounts are usually accounts that have been referred to a collection agency. These are the really annoying people who call you, and break a lot of rules and laws in doing so. By law they are not allowed to call you if you tell them not to. They don't care. All they care about is money. And BE CAREFUL if they want to negotiate, or if they promise you anything like removing an item in exchange for you making a payment or partial payment. Many times they will take your money and never remove an item from your credit report. They have purchased your debt from the original creditor for somewhere around 30-50 cents on the dollar, so they will try to recoup those funds, and then they'll disappear. I will tell you exactly how to deal with them in a moment.

3) Unsatisfactory accounts are accounts that have "late pays", where you are (or were) 30-90 days late on a payment, but have not yet been referred to a collection agency.

Now first things first, do not get upset or emotional. It is well-known that credit reports contain errors over 50% of the time. So you may even see things that are absolutely false. Or you may see some ridiculous $10 collection account you've never heard of, from many years ago. We will get everything removed in due time, so don't worry. Its just a game, and we will win.

In addition, I recommend IGNORING the recommendations on your credit report, where the credit bureaus give you "advice" on how to improve your score. Their recommendations are useless.

I'm not going to go into detail on everything on your report, because it doesn't matter. We just want the negative stuff gone, and that's it.

Please continue on the next page.

JUST DO THIS

There are 2 VERY SPECIFIC laws on your side. They are hidden in between hundreds of pages of legal mumbo jumbo, in 2 documents called the Fair Credit Reporting Act and the Fair Debt Collection Practices Act.

1) The Fair Credit Reporting Act (FCRA) – this document explains the rules and laws that the credit bureaus have to abide by. This is what we will refer to when dealing with Experian, Transunion, and Equifax.

2) The Fair Debt Collection Practices Act – this document explains the rules and laws that your creditors and collection agencies are required to abide by. We will refer to it when dealing with credit card companies, banks, and collection agencies.

I always recommend using BOTH of the laws below when attacking your bad credit. This gives you a higher percentage chance of getting negative items removed the quickest. Here are the two hidden laws that will lead to your freedom, when combined with my detailed steps.

<u>FCRA Section 623(a)(3)</u>

§ 623. Responsibilities of furnishers of information to consumer reporting agencies [15 U.S.C. § 1681s-2]

(a) (3) Duty to provide notice of dispute. If the completeness or accuracy of any information furnished by any person to any consumer reporting agency is disputed to such person by a consumer, the person may not furnish the information to any consumer reporting agency without notice that such information is disputed by the consumer.

<u>FDCPA Section 807(8)</u>

§ 807. False or misleading representations [15 USC 1962e]

(8) Communicating or threatening to communicate to any person credit information which is known or which should be known to be false, including the failure to communicate that a disputed debt is disputed.

What the laws mean, and how they help you:

My advice is to not read the FCRA or FDCPA unless you want to be bored out of your mind for several hours. But if you do, you will probably notice there are a couple of other laws that could potentially help you. It doesn't matter. I ONLY use the two above and they work GREAT.

Here's how...

<u>PART 1:</u>

FDCPA 807(8): This law deals directly with banks, credit card companies and collection agencies.

The big key here is that they are required to contact the credit bureaus on your behalf, and to make sure they add a sentence to your credit report WITHIN 30 DAYS that says you have disputed the negative item in question.

The sentence would appear something like this: "Customer has disputed the validity of this item"

They <u>almost never</u> add the sentence. I repeat, over 90% of the time, they will not do it. And certainly not in time.

Sometimes they will do it within 60 days. But that's too bad for them, because by law, they MUST do it within 30 days. We will simply prove that they didn't do it within 30 days, and they will be liable to you for DAMAGES of up to $1,000 per occurrence.

It is important to note that you are allowed to dispute anything on your credit report. It technically doesn't matter if it is something you know to be true and accurate. The responsibility is on the creditor to maintain accurate records and to follow the law within the required time-frames.

The other great thing is, we will be asking the creditor some hard hitting questions, and requesting very specific information from them... such as copies of your cashed checks showing you actually paid something late (for late pays you want removed)... and sometimes we will even require that the creditor provide a copy of the contract you physically signed, agreeing to their payment terms when you opened the account. Of course almost no company has these records readily available. Especially within 30 days! And not to mention, many credit card agreements were "digitally signed" through a website. It would be very difficult for them to contact their IT department and produce a print-out showing evidence that you digitally signed something.

If you're beginning to notice, we are trying to be a PAIN IN THE BUTT. All they have to do to make us go away is remove the item(s) :). If they don't, it gets worse for them as you will see...

What I personally love most about part 1 is that there is a chain of custody. Meaning, there are more people involved, which results in a better chance of the required sentence not being added in time. You contact the bank, and they have to contact the credit bureau, and the credit bureau has to act in time.

But let's move on to PART 2 of the plan...I like to implement part 2 only if part 1 has failed.

I will explain more in the "sample letters" section where I have pre-written letters and instructions for you, with exact dates and timing.

PART 2:

FCRA 623(a)(c): This law is very similar to the FDCPA above – it requires the credit bureau to report that you have disputed something on your credit report, after you have contacted them directly. They will need to add the dispute sentence to your credit report.

The big key here again, is that the credit bureaus are required to add the sentence to your credit report WITHIN 30 DAYS, that says you have disputed an item.

They almost never do. Again, 9 times out of 10, they will not do it in time. And the same thing applies as it did in PART 1 - we will simply prove that they didn't do it within 30 days, and they will be liable to your for DAMAGES of up to $1,000 per occurrence.

Now before you get excited about winning $1,000 from the credit bureaus and creditors each time, think about this... what if you told them they could keep the $1,000 and instead permanently remove your bad credit mark(s)? What do you think they would do?

They will remove your bad credit mark. They do not want to pay you. They do not want to go on public record as having lost a court case to you. They do not want this publicized, and they do not want to send out a legal team. All they have to do is have an employee remove the item from your report. Done deal. If the credit bureau or creditor decided to play hardball and not remove the item, you can remind them of how easy it is to put out a press release. Imagine how many NEW disputes they will get from the thousands of other people who read your press release.

As a side note, you can always do a free press release online. Just google 'free press release' to find many services.

Oh and by the way, there is always a decent chance that disputing with the credit bureaus in general will get an item or 2 removed without even needing to worry about the dispute sentence getting added within 30 days. I've seen quite a few items fall off just from using my basic dispute letter.

Anyway, I will show you the EXACT details in a moment, in my "sample letters" section, on exactly how to complete all of the above, in order, using my pre-written letters for any situation.

PART 3:

If by some miracle, both the credit bureaus and your creditors DO add the disputed sentence to your credit reports within the 30 day time frame, we have another avenue. Keep in mind that 99.9% of the people reading this will never need to resort to this.

You will go down to your local courthouse and file a "Small claims Lawsuit". Depending on your state it typically costs $20-$75 to file a small claims suite, and it only takes a few minutes.

Now don't get nervous. You won't actually be going to court, needing a lawyer, or anything like that. Trust me. I've only seen 4 creditors show up in court when myself, clients, or friends have used the tactics above.

2 of those 4 just wanted to see if we would show up. They saw us and settled immediately, right there in the court room before any proceedings started. (agreeing to remove the bad credit marks).

Only 2 times have I actually seen anyone have to even speak to the small claims judge.

And guess what? We won! Because while the creditor argued that the debts were true, we argued that we weren't here to decide whether or not the debts were true. We were simply there because the creditor failed to abide by FDCPA Section 807(8). The judge agreed, and the creditors lost.

The result: Filing fees reimbursed AND removal of the negative items!

One other advantage of small claims action is this: the creditor or credit bureau is required to COME TO YOU. Meaning they will need to fly out their legal people to your location to defend themselves. That would be a great expense for them. Given that small claims actions are not allow to cover attorney fees, if they send a legal team, even if they won, you would not be liable to pay their attorney fees.

To find the small claims court nearest you, simply do a Google search for "small claims court" and follow the directions, as each state is different. Sometimes they charge you more depending on how much you are suing for. So you may want to just do the minimum, since the goal is not to win any money anyway.

Please continue on the next page.

SAMPLE LETTERS

IMPORTANT – You must send any of the letters you use below via CERTIFIED MAIL, with a return receipt requested. This will not only ensure its delivery, but you will have a documented time of when it was received.

This is very important because we are going to nail the credit bureaus and creditors to that 30 day time-frame required by law. As soon as they sign for your letter, the 30 day clock starts ticking, and you will have a receipt of when they signed for it.

On DAY 31 you will print out a new copy of your credit reports, and they will be time & date stamped as well, from http://creditsecret.org/scores/. That is all of the evidence you need. Even if they add the sentence on the very next day, they've already broken the law.

NOTE: I have notes and things like (your name here) in the letters below. Make sure you proofread your letters and see that you've made all of the necessary edits where your own personal information is required. It would be pretty embarrassing if you left my notes, and the receiver likely wouldn't take you seriously.

My notes that you need to edit will have a yellow highlight like this.

Lastly, DO NOT sign any letters you send. You do not want your signature being compared, and used against you later, if they do happen to find your original contract.

Part 1, Letter #1 – (Send directly to the bank or agency that reported a derogatory or collection item to the credit bureaus)

Date

Your Name and Address

Name and Address of original bank/creditor (address shown on your credit report)

Re: Acct # 000-000-000-000

To Whom It May Concern:

This letter is regarding account # 000-000-000-000, which you claim (insert a derogatory condition here, such as "I owe $200.00" or "my account was charged off $800"). This is a formal notice that your claim is disputed.

I am requesting validation, made pursuant to the Fair Debt Collection Practices Act. Please note that I am requesting "validation"; that is competent evidence bearing my signature, showing that I have (or ever had) some contractual obligation to pay you. Please also be aware that any negative mark found on my credit reports (including Experian, Transunion and Equifax) from your company or any company that you represent, for a debt that I don't owe, is a violation of the Fair Debt Collection Practices Act; therefore if you cannot validate the debt, you must request that all credit reporting agencies delete the entry.

Pending the outcome of my investigation of any evidence that you submit, you are instructed to take no action that could be detrimental to any of my credit reports.

Failure to respond within 30 days of receipt of this certified letter will result in small claims legal action against your company at my local venue. I will be seeking a minimum of $5,000 in damages for:

1) Defamation

2) Negligent Enablement of Identity Fraud

3) Violation of the Fair Debt Collection Practices Act (including but not limited to Section 807-8)

You will be required to appear in a court venue local to me, in order to formally defend yourself.

For the purposes of 15 USC 1692 et seq., this Notice has the same effect as a dispute to the validity of the alleged debt and a dispute to the validity of your claims.

Please Note: This notice is an attempt to correct your records, and any information received from you will be collected as evidence should any further action be necessary. This is a request for information only, and is not a statement, election, or waiver of status.

My contact information is as follows:

Your Name (printed or typed, not signed)
SSN
Address

P.S. Please be aware that dependent upon your response, I may be detailing any potential issues with your company via an online public press release, including documentation of any potential small claims action.

Part 1 Letter # 2A (Send this 2nd letter only if you receive a letter back from a creditor in reply to letter # 1, saying your account was verified as "legitimate")

Date

Your Name and Address

Name and Address of original bank/creditor (address shown on your credit report)

Re: Acct # 000-000-000-000

To Whom It May Concern:

This letter is in response to your recent claim regarding account # 000-000-000-000, which you claim to have verified (insert a derogatory condition here, such as "I owe $200.00" or "my account was charged off $800").

Yet again, you have failed to provide me with a copy of any viable evidence, bearing my signature, showing the account is being reported accurately.

Be advised that the description of the procedure used to determine the accuracy and completeness of the information is hereby requested.

Additionally, please provide the name, address, and telephone number of each person who personally verified this alleged account, so that I can inquire about how they "verified" without providing any proof, bearing my signature.

I am again formally requesting a copy of any documents, bearing my signature, showing that I have a legally binding contractual obligation to pay you the alleged amount.

An employee looking at their computer screen, seeing my name listed in their database is NOT verification or validation of any alleged debt.

Be aware that I am making a final goodwill attempt to have you clear up this matter. The listed item is entirely inaccurate and incomplete, and represents a very serious error in your reporting.

with the FTC and the Attorney General's office, should you continue in your non-compliance of federal laws under the Fair Debt Collection Practices Act. I further remind you that you may be liable for your willful non-compliance as per FDCPA **§ 807. False or misleading representations [15 USC 1962e]**

Failure on your behalf to provide a copy of any alleged contract or other instrument bearing my signature will result in a small claims action against your company. I will be seeking $5,000 in damages for the following:

1) Defamation

2) Negligent Enablement of Identity Fraud

3) Violation of the Fair Credit Reporting Act

You will be required to appear in a court venue local to me, in order to formally defend yourself.

My contact information is as follows:

Your Name (printed or typed, not signed)
SSN
Address

P.S. Please be aware that dependent upon your response, I may be detailing any potential issues with your company via an online public press release, including documentation of any potential small claims action.

Part 1 Letter # 2b (Send this 2nd letter only if you DO NOT hear back from a creditor in reply to letter #1)

Date

Your Name and Address

Name and Address of original bank/creditor (address shown on your credit report)

Re: Acct # 000-000-000-000

To Whom It May Concern:

This letter is a follow up to my original letter dated (date) regarding an inaccuracy on my credit reports, regarding account # 000-000-000-000, which you claim (insert a derogatory condition here, such as "I owe $200.00" or "my account was charged off $800").

By not replying in a timely manner to my initial letter on (date), you have not only violated federal law, but you have also failed to provide me with a copy of any viable evidence, bearing my signature, showing the account is being reported accurately.

Be aware that I am making a final goodwill attempt to have you clear up this matter. The listed item is entirely inaccurate and incomplete, and represents a very serious error in your reporting.

I am maintaining a careful record of my communications with you for the purpose of filing a complaint with the FTC and the Attorney General's office, should you continue in your non-compliance of federal laws under the Fair Debt Collection Practices Act. I further remind you that you may be liable for your willful non-compliance, as per FDCPA **§ 807. False or misleading representations [15 USC 1962e]**

As you have now violated federal law, by not properly investigating within the required timeframe, and I have evidence of such, via certified mail receipts, you must now remove the item. Any other action (or in-action) on your behalf will result in a small claims action against your company.

I will be seeking $5,000 in damages for the following:
1) Defamation
2) Negligent Enablement of Identity Fraud
3) Violation of the Fair Credit Reporting Act

You will be required to appear in a court venue local to me, in order to formally defend yourself.

My contact information is as follows:

Your Name (printed or typed, not signed)
SSN
Address

P.S. Please be aware that dependent upon your response, I may be detailing any potential issues with your company via an online public press release, including documentation of any potential small claims action.

Part 1, Letter # 3 (send if your creditor responds with "proof" of your original signature – but wait until day 31 and make sure they have not marked the item as "disputed" on your credit reports)

Date

Your Name and Address

Name and Address of original bank/creditor (address shown on your credit report)

Re: Acct # 000-000-000-000

To Whom It May Concern:

This letter is a follow up to my original letter dated (date) regarding an inaccuracy on my credit reports, regarding account # 000-000-000-000, which you claim (insert a derogatory condition here, such as "I owe $200.00" or "my account was charged off $800").

Upon further investigation, I have retained new copies of my credit reports, and noticed that you did not furnish the credit bureaus with the required disclosure, within the period required by law. You are required by federal law to place a "notice of dispute" on my account within 30 days of my dispute, which you signed for on (date). I have retained a copy of your signature and date of receipt, as well as a timestamped copy of my credit reports, showing that you have violated the Fair Credit Reporting Act, Section 623(a)(3) by not placing the disclosure within the required 30 day period.

Be aware that I am making a final goodwill attempt to have you clear up this matter. The listed item is entirely inaccurate and incomplete, and represents a very serious error in your reporting. Additionally you have broken federal law by not placing the notice of dispute onto my credit reports within the time required by law.

I am maintaining a careful record of my communications with you for the purpose of filing a complaint with the FTC and the Attorney General's office, should you continue in your non-compliance of federal laws under the Fair Credit Reporting Act.

I further remind you that you may be liable for your willful non-compliance, as per FCRA 623(a)(3) - Responsibilities of furnishers of information to consumer reporting agencies [15 U.S.C. 1681s-2]

(3) Duty to provide notice of dispute. If the completeness or accuracy of any information furnished by any person to any consumer reporting agency is disputed to such person by a consumer, the person may not furnish the information to any consumer reporting agency without notice that such information is disputed by the consumer.

(B) Time of Notice
(I) The notice required under subparagraph (A) shall be provided to the customer prior to, or no later than 30 days after, furnishing the negative information to a consumer reporting agency described in section 603(p).

As you have violated federal law, by not properly providing the credit bureaus with proper notice within the required timeframe, and I have evidence of such, via certified mail receipts, you must now remove the item. Any other action (or in-action) on your behalf will result in a small claims action against your company.

I will be seeking $5,000 in damages for the following:

1) Defamation
2) Negligent Enablement of Identity Fraud
3) Violation of the Fair Credit Reporting Act

You will be required to appear in a court venue local to me, in order to formally defend yourself.

My contact information is as follows:

Your Name (printed or typed, not signed)
SSN
Address

P.S. Please be aware that dependent upon your response, I may be detailing any potential issues with your company via an online public press release, including documentation of any potential small claims action.

Part 1, Letter # 4 (send if you have not heard back from the creditor, or if they continue to "verify" the item without proof)

Date

Your Name and Address

Name and Address of original bank/creditor (address shown on your credit report)

Re: Acct # 000-000-000-000

To Whom It May Concern:

This letter is a follow up to my original letter dated (date) regarding an inaccuracy on my credit reports, regarding account # 000-000-000-000, which you claim (insert a derogatory condition here, such as "I owe $200.00" or "my account was charged off $800").

Yet again, you have failed to provide me with a copy of any viable evidence submitted by (Name of creditor).

Given that I believe you are acting in bad faith, and have not complied with the Federal Trade Commission (see 15 USC 41, et seq.), I have filed a Small Claims lawsuit against you. (see attached lawsuit)

I have maintained careful records of your actions, and you are now required to appear at (insert courthouse and address) on (date)

I am seeking $5,000 in damages for:

1) Defamation
2) Negligent Enablement of Identity Fraud
3) Violation of the Fair Credit Reporting Act

Prior to our court date on (date) if you should decide to correct your records and remove the negative and false item in question, please contact me at the address below, and I will subsequently drop the lawsuit.

My contact information is as follows:

Your Name (printed or typed, not signed)
SSN
Address

P.S. Please be aware that dependent upon your response, I may be detailing any potential issues with your company via an online public press release, including documentation of any potential small claims action.

Part 2, Letter # 1 (This is Your Original Dispute with the Credit Bureaus Directly – ONLY send this if you have not had success with the 4 letters above in Part 1)

Your Name

Your Address

Experian, Transunion, or Equifax

Address

Date

RE: Social Security Number: 000-00-0000

To Whom It May Concern:

I have recently been informed that there is negative information reported by (name of bank or creditor) in the file you maintain under my Social Security number. Upon ordering a copy of my credit report, I see an entry from this company listing (insert a derogatory condition here, such as "I owe $200.00" or "my account was charged off $800") in (month/year).

I am unaware of (insert a derogatory condition here, such as "owing $200.00" or "having a charge off") with this company.

Please validate this information with (name of creditor) and provide me with copies of any documentation associated with this account, bearing my signature. In the absence of any such documentation bearing my signature, I formally request that this information be immediately deleted from the credit file you maintain under my Social Security number.

Please note that you have 30 days to complete this investigation, as per the **Fair Credit Reporting Act section 623(a)(3)**, and I am keeping careful record of your actions.

Failure to respond satisfactorily within 30 days of receipt of this certified letter will result in a small claims action against your company. I will be seeking $5,000 in damages for:

1) Defamation
2) Negligent Enablement of Identity Fraud
3) Violation of the Fair Credit Reporting Act

You will be required to appear in a court venue local to me, in order to formally defend yourself.

My contact information is as follows:

Your Name (printed or typed, not signed)
SSN
Address

P.S. Please be aware that dependent upon your response, I may be detailing any potential issues with your company via an online public press release, including documentation of any potential small claims action.

Part 2, Letter # 2A (Send this if you receive a letter back from the credit bureau, saying your account was verified as "legitimate")

Your Name

Your Address

Experian, Transunion, or Equifax

Address

Date

RE: Social Security Number: 000-00-0000

To Whom It May Concern:

This letter is in response to your recent claim that (Name of creditor) has verified that I have an unpaid debt with them.

Yet again, you have failed to provide me with a copy of any viable evidence submitted by (Name of creditor).

Be advised that the description of the procedure used to determine the accuracy and completeness of the information is hereby requested, to be provided within fifteen (15) days of the completion of your re-investigation.

Additionally, please provide the name, address, and telephone number of each person contacted at (Name of creditor) regarding this alleged account. I am formally requesting a copy of any documents provided (Name of creditor), bearing my signature, showing that I have a legally binding contractual obligation to pay them the amount claimed.

An employee looking at their computer screen, seeing my name listed in their database is NOT verification or validation of any alleged debt.

Be aware that I am making a final goodwill attempt to have you clear up this matter. The listed item is entirely inaccurate and incomplete, and represents a very serious error in your reporting.

Failure to comply with federal regulations by credit reporting agencies are investigated by the Federal Trade Commission (see 15 USC 41, et seq.). I am maintaining a careful record of my communications with you for the purpose of filing a complaint with the FTC and the Attorney General's office, should you continue in your non-compliance. I further remind you that, as in Wenger v. Trans Union Corp., No. 95-6445 (C.D.Cal. Nov. 14, 1995), you may be liable for your willful non-compliance.

Failure to respond satisfactorily within 30 days of receipt of this certified letter will result in a small claims action against your company. I will be seeking $5,000 in damages for:

1) Defamation
2) Negligent Enablement of Identity Fraud
3) Violation of the Fair Credit Reporting Act

You will be required to appear in a court venue local to me, in order to formally defend yourself.

My contact information is as follows:

Your Name (printed or typed, not signed)
SSN
Address

P.S. Please be aware that dependent upon your response, I may be detailing any potential issues with your company via an online public press release, including documentation of any potential small claims action.

Part 2, Letter # 2B (Send this letter to the credit bureau if you do not get any response from letter #1)

Your Name

Your Address

Experian, Transunion, or Equifax

Address

Date

RE: Social Security Number: 000-00-0000

To Whom It May Concern:

This letter is a follow up to my original letter dated (date) regarding an inaccuracy in your credit reporting, regarding account # 000-000-000-000, reported by (creditor), which claims (insert a derogatory condition here, such as "I owe $200.00" or "my account was charged off $800").

By not replying in a timely manner to my initial letter on (date), you have not only violated federal law, but you have also failed to provide me with a copy of any viable evidence, bearing my signature, showing the account is being reported accurately.

Be aware that I am making a final goodwill attempt to have you clear up this matter. The listed item is entirely inaccurate and incomplete, and represents a very serious error in your reporting.

Failure to comply with federal regulations by credit reporting agencies are investigated by the Federal Trade Commission (see 15 USC 41, et seq.). I am maintaining a careful record of my communications with you for the purpose of filing a complaint with the FTC and the Attorney General's office, should you continue in your non-compliance. I further remind you that, as in Wenger v. Trans Union Corp., No. 95-6445 (C.D.Cal. Nov. 14, 1995), you may be liable for your willful non-compliance.

As you have now violated federal law, by not properly investigating within the required timeframe, and I have evidence of such, via certified mail receipts, you must now remove the item. Any other action (or in-action) on your behalf will result in a small claims action against your company.

I will be seeking $5,000 in damages for:

1) Defamation
2) Negligent Enablement of Identity Fraud
3) Violation of the Fair Credit Reporting Act

You will be required to appear in a court venue local to me, in order to formally defend yourself.

My contact information is as follows:

Your Name (printed or typed, not signed)
SSN
Address

P.S. Please be aware that dependent upon your response, I may be detailing any potential issues with your company via an online public press release, including documentation of any potential small claims action.

Part 2, Letter # 3 (send if you have not heard back from the credit bureau, or if they have continued to "verify" the item without proof)

Your Name

Your Address

Experian, Transunion, or Equifax

Address

Date

RE: Social Security Number: 000-00-0000

To Whom It May Concern:

This letter is my final communication in response to your reporting error, reported to you by (Name of creditor) for account # (insert acct # here).

I have repeatedly asked for evidence to support your reporting, but yet again, you have failed to provide me with a copy of any viable evidence submitted by (Name of creditor), substantiating their claims.

Given that I believe you are acting in bad faith, and have not complied with the Federal Trade Commission (see 15 USC 41, et seq.), I have filed a Small Claims lawsuit against you. (see attached lawsuit).

I have maintained careful records of your actions, and you are now required to appear at (insert courthouse and address) on (date).

I am seeking $5,000 in damages for:

1) Defamation
2) Negligent Enablement of Identity Fraud
3) Violation of the Fair Credit Reporting Act

Prior to our court date on (date) if you should decide to correct your records and remove the negative and false item in question, please contact me at the address below, and I will subsequently drop the lawsuit.

My contact information is as follows:

Your Name (printed or typed, not signed)
SSN
Address

P.S. Please be aware that dependent upon your response, I may be detailing any potential issues with your company via an online public press release, including documentation of any potential small claims action.

SMALL CLAIMS ACTION (PART 3 - SCARE TACTIC - IF NECESSARY)

If you've taken all of the above steps, with unfavorable results, you still have one, VERY POWERFUL final resort. The method is to file small claims suits against the credit bureau or creditor in question. Don't worry! It is much easier than it sounds. Most of the time they won't even put up a fight! They will settle. They will not show up in court. Not only will they delete your record, sometimes they will actually pay you a cash settlement.

After all, they benefit nothing by reporting your negative information. When they are threatened financially, they usually settle for removal in exchange for you dropping the suit.

All you need to do is go down to your local court and ask for the proper form, or you can download and print it from their website. Just Google "small claims court" and the one nearest you should appear in the search results. Each state is different, so just follow their simple instruc-tions on the website.

Don't forget, if the original bank failed to validate and show proof of a debt to YOU, how could the credit bureau possibly be verifying these debts!? They can't. This is because they verify the debts by contacting a clerk at the company who says, "Yes, I see the debt listed on our computer." They consider that "verification". But the courts do NOT consider that proper verification.

You will have many little known case laws to back you up. This is the stuff that they don't want anyone to know!

What you can file suit against the <u>credit bureaus</u> for:

"negligent and willful failure to reinvestigate the disputed entries in violation of sections 611(a), 616, and 617 of the FCRA, 15 U.S.C. §§ 1681i(a), 1681n, 1681o"

A copy of a similar lawsuit where Transunion was found liable:

FindLaw.com – In the search box enter some-thing in reference to: "Cushman v. Trans Union Corp., 920 F. Supp. 80 (E.D. Pa. 1996) or Cush-man v. Trans Union Corp., 115 F.3d 220 (3d Cir. 1997)"

Some other cases you may want to reference are:

Richardson v. Fleet Bank of Massachusetts – the court held that the company failed to follow reasonable procedures by relying on creditors for accurate credit information because the company had reason to know of the dispute between the consumer and the company.

Bryant v. TRW – the Defendant consumer reporting agency unsuccessfully argued that, under §607(b) of the FCRA, 15 U.S.C. §1681 et seq., it was not liable as a matter of law, for reports it issued in good faith, and as a result of inaccurate information provided to it by Plaintiff's creditors. The court held that Defendant was not free from liability when the credit reports at issue was not accurate. Once inaccu-racy was determined, defendant's agency procedures were determined to be not reason-able to ensure maximum possible accuracy, pursuant to §§607(b).

In Bryant v. TRW, Inc., 487 F.Supp. 1234, 1242-43 (E.D.Mich.1980), the district court awarded a consumer $8,000 for anguish resulting from denials of a mortgage due to inaccurate credit reports. The Sixth Circuit affirmed. 689 F.2d 72 (6th Cir.1982).

Stevenson v. TRW Inc., 987 F.2d 288, 293 (5th Cir. 1993). – "Allowing inaccurate information back onto a credit report after deleting it because it is inaccurate is negligent."

Fischl v. General Motors Acceptance Corp., 708 F.2d 143, 151 (5th Cir.1983). – Actual damages include humiliation or mental distress, even if the consumer has suffered no out-of-pocket losses.

In Pinner, 805 F.2d at 1265, the consumer was awarded $ 25,000 for mental distress because of the humiliation and embarrassment resulting from three credit denials and from lengthy dealings with the credit bureau. The court did, however, order a remittitur from the original jury award of $100,000 for mental distress.

Another consumer received $10,000 because of humiliation and embarrassment suffered from three denials of credit and from the fact that the credit bureau took several months to correct the credit report's inaccuracies. Thompson v. San Antonio Retail Merchants Ass'n, 682 F.2d 509, 513-14 (5th Cir.1982).

In Collins v. Retail Credit Co., 410 F.Supp. 924, 936 (E.D.Mich.1976), the court awarded a consumer $21,750 for embarrassment and humiliation.

In Morris v. Credit Bureau of Cincinnati, Inc., 563 F.Supp. 962, 969 (S.D.Ohio 1983), the consumer was awarded $10,000 for anguish and embarrassment even though, after he was denied credit, he explained the inaccuracies on his credit report and subsequently obtained credit.

In Millstone v. O'Hanlon Reports, Inc., 528 F.2d 829, 834-35 (8th Cir.1976), the Eighth Circuit upheld an award of $2,500 for mental anguish after an insurer canceled the consumer's policy because of an inaccurate credit report.

Ryan v. Trans Union Corp., Case No. 99 C 216, 2001 – "The court held that defendants were entitled to a partial award of attorney's fees from plaintiff under the FCRA to the extent that plaintiff filed oppositions to defendants' summary judgment motions knowing that he no longer had a valid claim."

What you can sue your creditors for:

§ 807. False or misleading representations [15 USC 1962e]

(8) Communicating or threatening to communicate to any person credit information which is known or which should be known to be false, including the failure to communicate that a disputed debt is disputed.

Another court case you can reference:

Spears/Brennan Appeal from the Marion Superior Court - The judge ruled the following:

"As discussed previously, an FDCPA claim has nothing to do with whether the underlying debt is valid. An FDCPA claim concerns the method of collecting the debt. It does not arise out of the transaction creating the debt [.] Azar, 874 F. Supp. at 1318. Footnote: See 15 U.S.C. § 1692k (governing civil liabil-ity under the Act).

Do a search at FindLaw.com for the case, and you will find documentation on it.

IMPORTANT: When you are filing a small claims suit against a company outside of your own state, you are required to put their "registered agent & address" on the form, instead of their office address. You can find the registered agent & address for any company by going to RegisteredAgentInfo.com

METHOD TO QUICKLY GET GOOD CREDIT LINES

Method 1: Piggybacking - A friend of mine named Tyler moved to the U.S. from Canada and had no credit. He asked his friend with awesome credit to add him onto his Platinum Amex account as an "authorized user". Tyler never even used the card and 6 months later his credit was 720.

This is because he is basically taking advantage of his friend's great credit. Tyler's friend basically vouched for him and the credit bureaus love that when it comes from a reputable person. A lot of 18-22 year olds do the same thing, piggybacking on their parent's accounts. Spouses also help each other out this way if one has better credit than the other.

By doing this, the authorized user receives a spillover of benefits of the main account holder's good credit, without ever actually needing to use the card.

FINAL NOTES / SUMMARY

• My 3-part approach is virtually unbeatable. You will win if you persist and follow my approach EXACTLY. Part 1 is dealing with the creditor directly. Part 2 is dealing with the credit bureaus directly. Part 3 is small claims action. Part 3 is almost never required, and is usually just a threat that works extraordinarily well.

• Don't forget to look on your credit reports for any missing entries or information. You may have several "good credit" entries that were NOT reported by one of your creditors or lenders. If you find this, contact your creditor and ask them to report the good accounts to all 3 credit bureaus if possible.

• Be organized! Keep good records of your documents and date receipts in file folders. Make sure to print out your credit reports exactly 31 days after the date shown on your certified mail receipts.

• It has been said that once you get an item deleted from your credit report, it can be placed back on your report at a later date. It is true that the credit bureaus often delete a negative item temporarily, if they haven't heard from your creditor after thirty days. If the creditor then reports after the thirty day period and "verifies" the negative item, the credit bureau will often reinsert it onto your credit report. This is known as a "soft delete." That is why it is imperative to get it in writing when a company agrees to remove a negative item. You can send a copy of that letter to the credit bureaus.

• Some creditors or collection agencies will negotiate with you for full or partial payment in exchange for removal of the bad listing on your credit report. This can come in handy on small items that you can afford to pay, like an old cable bill for $27. It isn't worth going to court over an amount like that. But make sure you get something in writing before you pay them. And before you accept their offer, ask them to report your account as "PAID AS AGREED" or to delete the listing altogether. DO NOT accept "Paid was Late", "Paid Collection", Paid P & L", or "Paid Charge Off". These are all very damaging entries on your report.

• There are some companies and websites advertising that they can create an entirely new credit history for you by getting the government to issue you a new Social Security Number #. This is 100% illegal - DON'T TRY IT!

WHAT TO DO AFTER MY METHOD FIXES YOUR CREDIT

Here are little-known tips and best practices I have learned directly from an officer who worked at the FICO company formerly known as "Fair Isaac". FICO provides the score that lenders use to evaluate whether or not you are credit-worthy.

1) Once you are approved for a credit card or credit line, regularly ask for a limit increase... at least 3 times per year. Credit limit increases are good, and they lower your overall percentage owed on your entire credit profile.

2) Do your best to pay off all credit cards and charge cards every month. This helps your score tremendously.

3) Get a business credit card. If you do not own a business, you can easily create one at LegalZoom.com for less than $200. If you do anything of value outside of your normal 9 to 5 job, even if you sell baked goods and only make a few hundred dollars a year... incorporate a small business... at least on paper. It will open up many more credit opportunities.

4) Charge cards are better for your credit than regular credit cards. Charge cards are those like American Express, which require you to pay the full balance off every month.

5) Inquiries can hurt your score, especially if you apply for several credit cards in a short period of time. However, the same is NOT true with auto loans or home loans. You can apply for as many auto loans or home loans as you want within a 45 day period, and it will all only count as 1 inquiry. (1 for autos and 1 for homes)

6) Do not close any credit cards you have paid off. It looks better to have existing, open accounts with a zero balance.

FREQUENTLY ASKED QUESTIONS

(these are from actual customers and include the response we sent to them)

Question: 'I'm looking at the credit reports and all my accounts end with 'XXXX' so they are obviously disguising last 4 digits. Do I need to send in my complete account # on my letters? How do I get complete the complete number?'

Answer: 'In your letter, include whatever numbers you do know, and then use X's for the remainder like they do. They will be able to identify you by your social and address anyway'

Question: 'All credit bureaus added the dispute statement to my credit report before the 31 days. What do I do now?'

Answer: 'It sounds like you skipped to step 2 – sending letters to the credit bureaus, instead of completing step 1 – sending letters to the creditors first. It's much easier for the credit bureaus to place the dispute sentence on your report, than it is for your creditors. So now what I would do is go back and do step 1. The creditors need to provide you with proof of your original contract. But unfortunately, since you went out of order this will likely end up being a case where you will need to file small claims and then they will cave or not show up in court. But there is still a chance that the creditors may delete just based on your letters and threats, or if you have them served with a small claims suit. This is why it is important to follow the steps as they are laid out and not skip ahead, otherwise it hurts your chances a bit and causes you more paperwork.'

Question: 'I've been sending out the letters and receiving responses from some and being ignored by others. So I'm at the point where I have no other option but to sue them. I have a few questions about that: 1. What can I actually sue for? The Credit Reporting agencies are telling me that they legally don't have to send me this stuff. 2. Can I sue the creditors for not sending me proof that I had an agreement with them?

Answer: 'Make sure you read the section called "What you can sue for". And also ignore anything the bureaus say about what you can and cannot do. They'll have their day to explain in court if they show up. Its more likely that you serve them a copy of the upcoming case and they're not going to fly a team of lawyers out. Which means you win by default.'

Question: 'For a Tax Lien dispute (Public Record), what is the appropriate "derogatory condition" to add to the first sentence of Part 1 Letter 1? i.e. This letter is regarding case #00000 which you claim (derogatory condition $$$).'

Answer: 'Which you claim "I have a tax lien for X amount of $$" '

Question: 'I live in Canada and would like to know if the laws that allow us to change our credit scores are the same. We also have TransUnion and Equifax, but not Experian. Any knowledge on Canadian law would be of help. Thanks.'

Answer: 'You would need to look to see if Canada has something similar to our fair credit reporting act or our fair debt collection practices act. Our credit secret methods only work in the USA.'

Question: 'For the dispute letter to the credit bureaus, in addition to the creditors name, do we add the account number as well?'

Answer: 'Yes. If you only have a partial number, include that.'

Question: "Is it "Game Over" if they provide proof of my signature after the first letter?'

Answer: 'No because the law is that they need to mark it as disputed within 30 days regardless.'

Question: 'I was wondering if this can work for student loans?'

Answer: 'It can be applied to every type of negative account'

Question: 'Anyone have an issue with the credit report not including full account numbers?'

Answer: 'For account numbers, just put the same number they did, and include asterisks for the rest if they did. Your SS# will let them know how to find the account.

Question: 'Isn't there a statute of limitations?'

Answer: The following timelines are the maximum that a derogatory mark can remain on your credit report:

Late payments: 7 years
Bankruptcies: 7 years for completed Chapter 13 bankruptcies and 10 years for Chapter 7 bankruptcies.
Foreclosures: 7 years
Collections: Generally, about 7 years, depending on the age of the debt being collected.
Public Record: Generally 7 years, although unpaid tax liens can remain indefinitely.

Question: "Question on Judgments - can the system be used for credit card companies that have won a judgment against me? Is it still the same process starting with the letters to the original creditor? Does the fact that they went to court and got the judgment change what they need to provide me with if requested?"

Answer: "You actually can dispute a judgment. You can dispute anything. The key is whether or not they mark it as "disputed" on your credit report within the required time. For instance, I once had a judgment from a gardening company who continued to garden at a house I moved out of 6 months prior. And apparently the new homeowner let them go ahead and garden without paying.

Then one day I found out I had a judgment for 6 months of gardening work – about $1200. I was never served, nor did I have a contract, or owe these people money. So I most certainly disputed it and ultimately got it removed."

Question: "I received my first response from one of the collection agencies stating that there is no law that obligates them to provide me with signed contracts, copies of state licenses, etc... The letter also said that they requested the credit bureau update my account as "disputed" and that my account was verified, but the proof they provided me was a bill with my SSN, address, and phone number so I'm guessing at this point I should proceed with letter 2A?

Answer: "Yes, you are correct. If it eventually goes to small claims, which it likely won't, it would be pretty interesting for them to show up and basically say "your honor he owes us money, we don't have a contract, but we pinky swear he owes us"

Question: "I filed a small claims lawsuit against a creditor recently. They responded with a motion to move the case from my local county to a US District Court in Richmond, VA (about an hour away from me) citing that I am alleging violations of the FDCPA and that is a federal law and therefore should be heard in federal court. Anyone dealt with this? Any help would be greatly appre-ciated"

Answer: "Here is a great thread about this rare circumstance, and how to keep it in small claims: http://www.creditinfocenter.com/community/topic/277129-small-claims-suit-being-moved-tofederal-court/ "

Question: "If I have 10 items to dispute, can I send 10 letters with 1 dispute per letter all at the same time? Or should I do 1, wait the 31 days, then do another? It could take eons that way, right?"

Answer: "Your goal is to have the highest percentage possible for them to make a mistake. Do 10 separate disputes. Clerical errors and your letters getting tossed into a pile, are both your friend."

Question: "I received pretty much an entire "book' from a collector with actual proof of signatures etc...but they completely disregarded the fact that I disputed the debt and there is no indication on my report(s) that it's been disputed, so where should I go from this point, wait the thirty days and file suit or should I send another letter?"

Answer: "Then they just broke the law. You should send the next letter, letting them know they have broken the law and that you intend to file a small claims suit. Or you can get more aggressive and go ahead and file the small claims suit. Then send them a copy of it, and let them know you are willing to drop the suit in exchange for them deleting the negative information."

Question: "What if a letter goes unclaimed at the PO box?"

Answer: "Google their physical address and send the letter to them there, via certified mail. Without the signature, it is going to be tough to prove they violated the 30 day rule. Plus it sounds like your future letters will go unanswered at that PO Box address."

Question: Is this repair method only for removing negative trade lines on the credit report or does it also work for removing things like judgments and bankruptcies as well?

Answer: Everything is fair game. For a bankruptcy, you would be using it on items that say "included in bankruptcy".

Question: How long will it take on average to take it to go from a 500 score to 750?

Answer: It depends on you doing things in a timely fashion and following the system exactly. My wife went from 588 to 781 in 3 months. But she went from 588 to 719 in about 45 days. I typically only talk about going up 100 points quickly. 250 points would likely take 3-6 months.

Question: Is this just temporary credit score increase? I negotiated my settlements with 10 credit cards and they whacked me for "settled for less than full" and "charge off". If your system is inquiry investigation/dispute and prove it, then these 20 may be removed during the investigations, but they will pop up back again when they are confirmed as legit, which they are. I have no legal way to say they are bogus as I did settle for less than full. So is it temporary?

Answer: This is not temporary - items are not removed during investigations. They are removed once you become too much of a pain in the butt to these creditors. Make it not worth their time to fight you. It only takes them a couple of minutes to delete your info. And that is permanent.

Also, as a side-note, you can in fact say that you do not recall something on your credit report, such as a negotiated settlement, a charge-off, etc. I don't recall many things, even things I did yesterday.

Question: Are your methods legal, or should I check with an attorney?

Answer: I am not a lawyer, so if you feel uneasy, feel free to ask one. But after having helped people for 13+ years, and based on myself going to court against Equifax, Experian, Transunion, and 9 collection agencies, this is 100% legal. I have won 13 cases, most by default – meaning they didn't show up.

Question: Will this work for student loans as well and if you are making payments on a delinquent account?

Answer: You can remove late payment(s), or an account altogether. Although if you were going to remove it altogether, that would be pretty tough if you're still paying on it. It sounds like the best option would be to remove the delinquency aspect of it.

Question: 'I sent out my letters for a few late payments on student loans and credit cards to hope-fully get them removed from a while back. I received a letter from Bank of America with no proof so I will send second letter, but Chase Student Loans actually sent me a copy of my signed loan document. Does this mean I have to go to small claims court now to get it removed?'

Answer: 'Even if they sent you proof of the contract, they still need to mark it as disputed on your credit reports within 30 days or they have broken the law.'

Scott Hilton's **CREDIT SECRET**

PROOF THIS WORKS

HERE'S WHAT FOLKS ARE SAYING ABOUT US ON FACEBOOK

YOU GET INSTANT ACCESS TO THIS PRIVATE GROUP!

Aimee M
November 12, 2015

Update: Wow!!!! after a disappointing drop in my credit score on Credit Karma a few days ago my Privacy Guard report was updated today. I had to blink to make sure I was seeing straight. My Experian score jumped 165 points in the last 30 days. Two collection accounts were deleted and 2 delinquencies were deleted. I'm feeling almost human again!

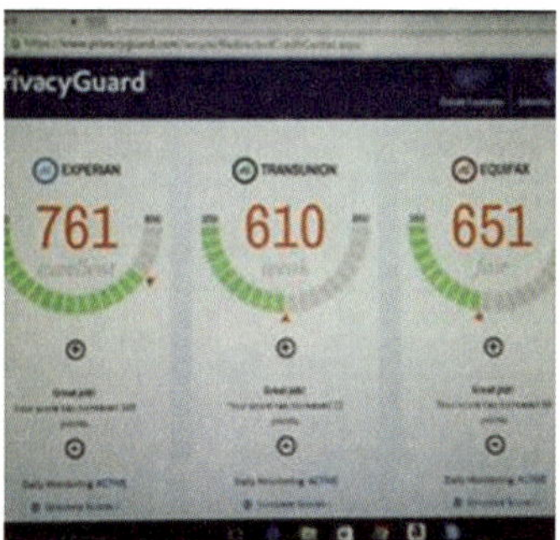

BOOM!

+100!

Bryan T
May 11, 2015

My Lowest Score Went Up 100 points in last week and a half. Every student loan I EVER had including the federal ones owed to the government came off...It looks like I never even went to college. LOL!

100% Succesful!

Amaya L celebrating success.
February 29 at 1:22pm · New York, NY

Look at this beautiful thing. Wow! My score went from low 600s to this amazing, almost 800 thing of beauty. And all it took was a few letters 😃

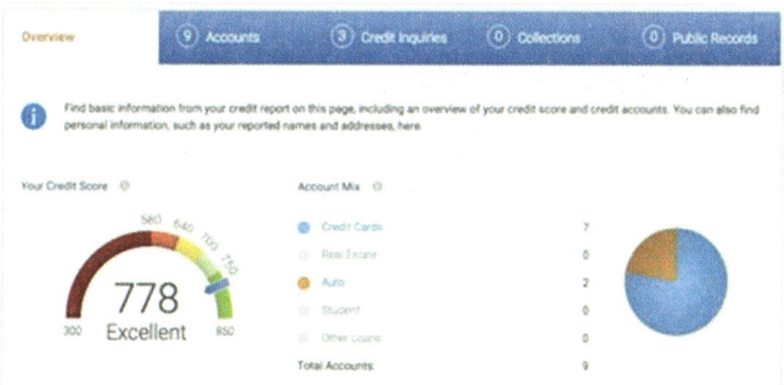

Like Comment

You, Desmond, Tanchra, Kris and 59 others

BOOM!

Jeremy S
January 6

So I had small claims court for a collection agency and they did not show up. Default Judgement for full $5,000. The Judge allowed me to explain and cut me off because of the default judgement. The fact of the matter is, if you question whether this information is accurate and reliable, the answer is YES!!! If it was not the Judge would have stopped me and dismissed the case. Hope this helps with people's question about small claims.

25 22 Comments

Darchae W
March 6 at 12:55pm

I started this group in December, been doing a lot of clean up with my credit checked my email this morning and saw my score has increased...i started in the low 600's...check me out now!! Still have more to clean up and workin on my hubbys but Im getting there!! #thisdoeswork #workinprogress

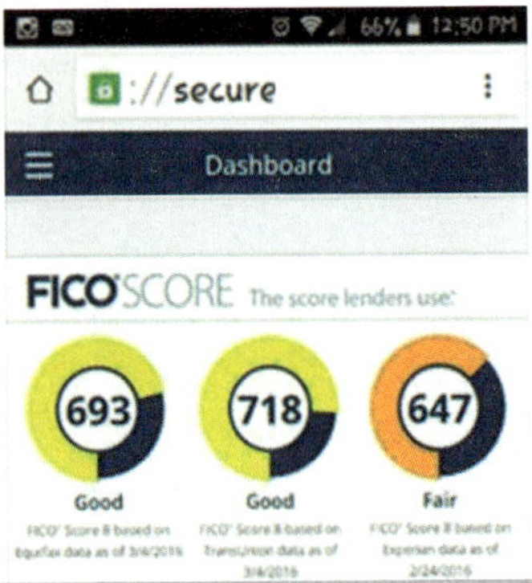

WHAM!

Jason C
December 3, 2015

WHAM!

Hi everyone. I just got approved for a credit card with a $10,000 limit!

Its with a local credit union. I'm amazed because just a few weeks ago my FICO score was 633. Turns out my score jumped up to 747!!

31 · 5 Comments

Like · Comment

Scott Hilton's **CREDIT SECRET**

100% Succesful!

Ernie B

May 1, 2015

Just got this in the mail today... Can you say bye bye judgement

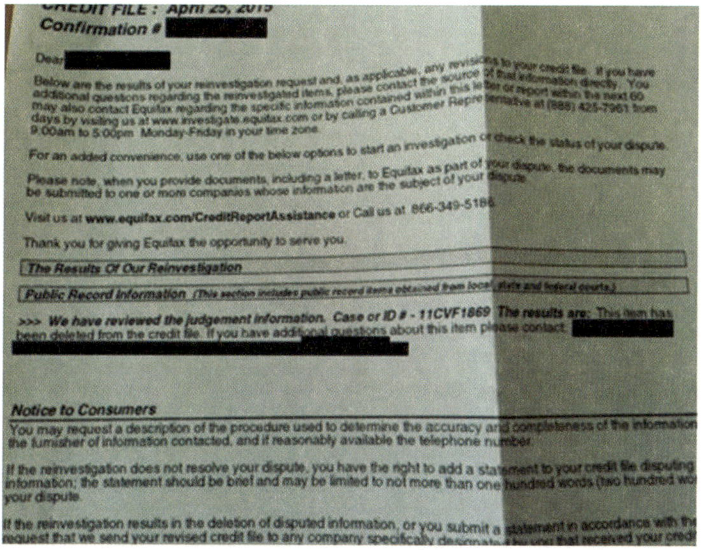

CREDIT FILE : April 25, 2015

Confirmation #

Dear

Below are the results of your reinvestigation request and, as applicable, any revisions to your credit file. If you have additional questions regarding the reinvestigated items, please contact the source of that information directly. You may also contact Equifax regarding the specific information contained within this letter or report within the next 60 days by visiting us at www.investigate.equifax.com or by calling a Customer Representative at (888) 425-7961 from 9:00am to 5:00pm Monday-Friday in your time zone.

For an added convenience, use one of the below options to start an investigation or check the status of your dispute.

Please note, when you provide documents, including a letter, to Equifax as part of your dispute, the documents may be submitted to one or more companies whose information are the subject of your dispute.

Visit us at **www.equifax.com/CreditReportAssistance** or Call us at 866-349-5186

Thank you for giving Equifax the opportunity to serve you.

The Results Of Our Reinvestigation

Public Record Information *(This section includes public record items obtained from local, state and federal courts.)*

>>> ***We have reviewed the judgement information. Case or ID # - 11CVF1869*** **The results are:** This item has been deleted from the credit file. If you have additional questions about this item please contact:

Notice to Consumers

You may request a description of the procedure used to determine the accuracy and completeness of the information the furnisher of information contacted, and if reasonably available the telephone number

If the reinvestigation does not resolve your dispute, you have the right to add a statement to your credit file disputing information; the statement should be brief and may be limited to not more than one hundred words (two hundred wo[rds] your dispute.

If the reinvestigation results in the deletion of disputed information, or you submit a statement in accordance with the request that we send your revised credit file to any company specifically designated by you that received your credi[t]

+100!

Joan M

October 13, 2015

For anyone who is feeling discouraged. This system REALLY works! My credit score is up to 708 from 602 in less than 3 months! YOU CAN DO IT!

Scott Hilton's CREDIT SECRET

Stefan J
October 4, 2015

BOOM!

Getting closer to my 800 credit score goal within a year! I still have one more account to get removed that's being a pain in the ass, but I will win and get it removed in the end! Once I get it removed and my new Amex card gets added to my credit report, this will surely raise my score closer to 800! Let's go!

BOOM!

Stefan J
March 21, 2015

Great Saturday. Just received a letter in the mail from Equifax that my judgement was deleted!

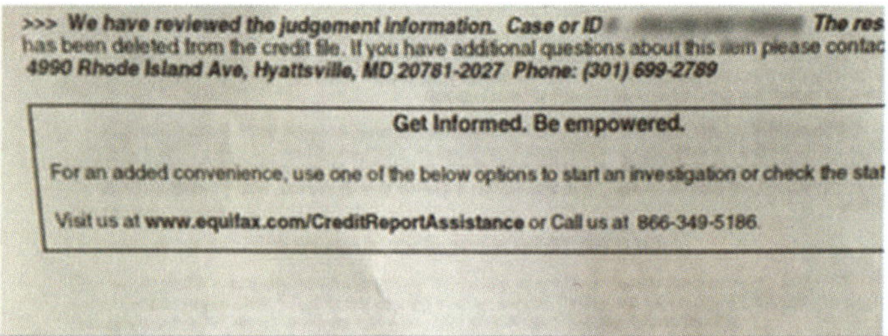
>>> *We have reviewed the judgement information. Case or ID* [redacted] *The res*
has been deleted from the credit file. If you have additional questions about this item please contac
4990 Rhode Island Ave, Hyattsville, MD 20781-2027 Phone: (301) 699-2789

Get Informed. Be empowered.

For an added convenience, use one of the below options to start an investigation or check the stat

Visit us at **www.equifax.com/CreditReportAssistance** or Call us at 866-349-5186

Shaiqiyah M feeling excited.
June 3, 2015

"I am so happy and grateful now, that I have EXCELLENT credit!"

I was just checking this site out and saw that another creditor has decided to comply and remove an account. I am very pleased!!! #creditsecret #removeitorpayme

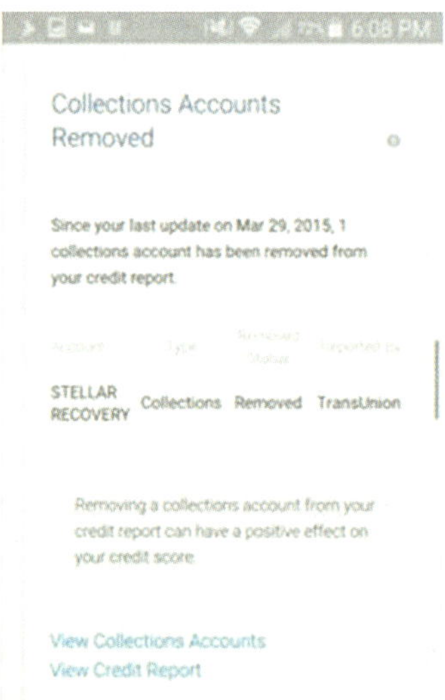

WHAM!